THE
METAL
DETECTIVE

2

The Adventures Continue

THE METAL DETECTIVE

2

The Adventures Continue

by Alan Rothman

Edited by Jeffrey Neal Rothman

SMALL BATCH BOOKS

AMHERST, MASSACHUSETTS

Designed by Carolyn Eckert

Illustrated by Daniela Frongia

Cover caricature of author by Mark Gennaro

Library of Congress Control Number: 2018930297

ISBN: 978-1-937650-91-9

SMALL
BATCH
BOOKS

493 SOUTH PLEASANT STREET

AMHERST, MASSACHUSETTS 01002

413.230.3943

SMALLBATCHBOOKS.COM

This book is dedicated to my wonderful grandchildren,
Cooper, Sloane, Henry, Owen, Isaac, Caroline, and Emma.

CONTENTS

ACKNOWLEDGMENTS

MY FIRST ATTEMPT at writing was a very rewarding experience. Many of my readers encouraged me to write a sequel; this dual book is the result of those requests.

I would first like to thank all those people who were kind enough to purchase my first book, *The Metal Detective: Treasures Lost and Friendships Found*, and write such wonderful reviews. Since its publication, I have appeared on television and the front pages of a few newspapers and have been asked to give presentations to audiences of all ages, ranging from five-year-olds to senior citizens.

On more than one occasion, I have been recognized as the Metal Detective on the beaches of Cape Cod and have become a minor celebrity of sorts. How strange it is that for all these years spent practicing as a CPA, aside from time spent with my clients, I have lived in obscurity.

I believe my wife, Myrna, is still struggling to get through my book, though she somehow is an active member of a book club that requires reading books of several hundred pages. Perhaps Myrna has heard my stories so many times that she feels she has been subjected to enough punishment.

It would be impossible to mention all the wonderful people that I've met, or all those who supported and encouraged me after the completion of my first book, but there are some individuals that I feel compelled to mention:

My mother, Edith, was by far my best customer; I believe she spent my future inheritance purchasing books for most of the people she has met over the past ninety-eight years.

I'd also like to acknowledge Don and Joy Nelson, who apparently hoped to ride my coattails toward celebrity status and also purchased numerous copies. The record single-day sales (twenty-three) on Amazon came as a direct result of the Nelsons' order.

I'd also like to note the support of the Red Jacket Beach management, Platinum Auto, The Great Island Bakery, The McConnell Group, and Wells Fargo Advisors, along with so many other business establishments that helped promote my first book by putting it on display for the public. I have been very fortunate to have friends both on and off the Cape offer *The Metal Detective* for sale, expecting no financial return, but simply extending their assistance in getting the book into the hands of as many readers as possible.

My sincere thanks for everyone's support.

—A. R.

Liam (center), with his mom and my grandson Owen, sees his name in print.

THE REUNION

FOR THOSE WHO HAVE READ MY FIRST BOOK, the finding of Liam's glasses is known as the impetus for my writing. I devoted my first vignette to Liam and the discovery of his glasses. Over the past two years, I unsuccessfully made numerous attempts to locate Liam and his family; I wanted them to know how important that chance meeting and the recovery of his glasses were to me.

Then one day, while searching for treasures at the Red Jacket Beach Resort, a man and a woman, whom I at first didn't recognize, approached me and said they knew me from somewhere, but weren't sure where. We got onto the subject of my being the Metal Detective, and I explained how finding a little boy's glasses changed my life.

To my confusion, they immediately pointed to a boy sitting nearby. It turned out, I was talking to Liam's parents, Scott and Maureen, and the boy was Liam!

I gave him a warm hug and told him that because so many people have read my book, he is, in a way, a celebrity in his own right. I presented Liam with an autographed book and now consider him a pen pal who may someday (I hope) join me in the hunt for treasures. The look of amazement on his face when he opened the book and saw his name in bold letters is something I will never forget. In hindsight, I think about how I happened to be metal detecting that day, two years after our first encounter, when Liam and his family were staying at the resort, and I imagine it was meant to be.

ON SHELVES AND AUTOGRAPHS

ONE DAY, I was asked to do a book signing at a local library with my son Jeffrey, who edited my first book. Much to my surprise, the book was so well received that it is now part of several library collections and is frequently signed out by the public.

There have been so many instances when people have mentioned to me that they've either written a book or always wanted to publish a book. Not an easy task, but with patience and support the dream can come true. Both Jeffrey and I have encouraged potential authors to feel free to contact us for suggestions as to how to fulfill their dream of being published.

✳ ✳ ✳

"Onwen" and me, at a signing at Yellow Umbrella Books, in Chatham, Massachusetts.

T ANOTHER BOOK SIGNING, my grandson Owen, who was four years old at the time, decided to join me. Owen, along with my other grandchildren, appears on the back cover of *The Metal Detective*. As I was about to autograph a book, the buyer stopped me. In a polite manner, she said, "I want him [Owen] to sign it because he will be famous some day, since he is on the cover."

"He really is just learning to spell his name and will make a mess," I replied.

Owen proceeded to write his name as "Onwen." She accepted the book and left with a smile on her face.

✳ ✳ ✳

Former NBA coach and friend Don Nelson and me, dual autographing.

I HAVE REPRESENTED professional athletes for most of my adult life and have been present on many occasions when fans ask them for autographs. I always wondered what made it so important that people would brave the elements of rain and snow just to get these treasured signatures. But now I willingly autograph my book whenever requested and ask each buyer who I should address my remarks to in their copy.

One unusual signing took place when an individual requested a joint session with myself and Don Nelson, a five-time Boston Celtics world champion and the NBA coach with the most career wins. Don is also a longtime friend and client of mine. I autographed my book while Don signed his No. 19 Celtics jersey.

That was a very special moment for both of us.

THE TREASURE HUNT

J EFF AND I REQUESTED A MEETING with the management of the Red Jacket Beach Resort to present our ideas for a children's pirate treasure hunt. Much to our delight, the resort purchased several junior metal detectors, along with gold and silver replica coins to bury in the sand. Thanks to our meeting on that cold winter's day, the first of what will hopefully be a yearly junior detective treasure-hunting program was launched on the beaches of Cape Cod.

THE PIED PIPER REDUX

CHILDREN OFTEN FOLLOW ME around like the pied piper. Being surrounded by the youngsters creates a challenge since they are constantly by my feet, just waiting to pounce on the metal source causing pings from my trusty little detector. My stamina, however, does not come close to equaling theirs. When I need a break, I tell them I will alert them with a whistle once I begin detecting again if that magic ping rings out. At that point, they can come running to see my find.

One afternoon at the beach, I told my followers that I needed a rest. Myrna was sitting at the water's edge and decided to take advantage of the rare occasion by taking a walk, leaving me to guard her pocketbook. An hour later, when Myrna hadn't returned, I figured she had forgotten where our chairs were. I whistled out to her so she could get her bearings, but instead, several sets of parents started laughing at me. I turned around to see at least a dozen children running out of the ocean toward me to see what I had found! "False alarm!" I yelled, but I was still almost trampled by the masses.

✳ ✳ ✳

ONE DAY WHILE METAL DETECTING AT THE RESORT, with several children following me (with their parents' permission, of course), I came upon what the youngsters had always hoped to see—"pirate's treasure."

My trusty, rusty detector put out a very strong signal, indicating that something metallic hid beneath the sand. Each scoop brought several gold and silver pirate's coins, much to the kids' amazement.

The children started to fantasize about what they would be able to buy with their loot; the list included a pet elephant, a pet giraffe, and a hotel with many rooms. They also dreamed of a house with bunk beds for each member of their family.

As the pied piper, I made sure that all of the kids went back to their parents with coins in hand. One mother actually believed that we had found a real treasure chest, when, in fact, we'd inadvertently dug up the planted coins from the resort's scavenger hunt that Jeff, my son and editor, and I had suggested as an activity. I suppose someday I will have to reimburse the management for what is now technically their lost treasure.

The scene of the find, at Nantucket's Children's Beach.

PIRATE'S TREASURE

A S I WALK THE BEACHES with my detector, the children who see me almost always ask, "What are you looking for?" "Pirate treasure," I answer, jokingly.

Surprisingly, one day at Children's Beach in Nantucket, this came true. As I searched in front of a lifeguard stand, a loud ping indicated a significant metal object several feet under the sand. The two female lifeguards asked if I planned to dig up whatever was there, and I said no, since it was far too deep for me, and my back ached from a long day of detecting. Fortunately, lifeguards have a piece of equipment that came in handy this particular day: a shovel. The two young ladies asked if they could try and locate the object. I agreed and insisted that anything we found would be split three ways.

Soon the area was inundated with curious beachgoers awaiting the discovery of a possible treasure. At approximately three feet deep, the shovel hit a metal box. It was locked, so I shook the box and, amazingly, there was something rattling inside. Everyone was stunned, thinking this might actually be pirate's booty. With the lifeguard shovel, I was able to force open this wonderful find. It popped open, revealing a child's plastic pirate sword. Now it really got interesting. Next came a plastic replica of Captain Hook's famous hook, followed by a miniature lighthouse with Nantucket spelled out on its side.

The adults surrounding the lifeguards and I knew right away that this treasure chest was probably planted a few years ago, but the children to this day may very well believe that they were witnessing the discovery of a real pirate's chest.

I called Myrna, who was quite upset that I interrupted her while she was shopping. I told her to come to the beach as soon as she could to see my find. "This is what I came here for?!" This was a great way to get her mind off shopping even though it only lasted a short time. The news spread quickly on the island among all the lifeguards, and I became a celebrity for the day at every beach I went to.

THE LANYARD

ONE UNUSUAL DISCOVERY was a lanyard with multiple keys lying on the sand. The area in which I found it is seldom used by swimmers and is not conducive for a day of enjoyment at the beach. Inscriptions on the lanyard indicated that it must have belonged to army personnel—quite possibly the remnant of maneuvers performed along the coastline.

After doing some research, my best guess is that the keys fell out of a helicopter. I made many attempts to try and locate the owner, but was ultimately unsuccessful. My treasure chests are filled with many such unclaimed objects that I now claim as my own.

THE FIRST
METAL DETECTOR

IN 1881, PRESIDENT JAMES GARFIELD was the target of an attempted assassination and was shot in the back. When the surgeons were unable to locate the bullet, Alexander Graham Bell rushed to the president's bedside with his newly invented metal detector, hoping to use it to locate the bullet, but was unsuccessful.

Within a few months, Garfield died. It was determined that the bed that he had been lying on had metal springs, and the detector used by Bell could not discriminate between the signals of the bullet and the springs. Today, a simple X-ray would reveal the bullet.

SHARING MY HOBBY
My Audience

HOW VERY DIFFERENT it is to make a presentation to five-year-olds versus the older generation. Both audiences are intrigued by my treasures, but when it comes to the question-and-answer period, it is like night and day!

The children basically want to know if they can take home some of the treasures, while the older audience seems to be more interested in the twenty-year-old blonde I found while detecting on Maui. There was one instance in which I did mention the blonde to the youngsters, but all I saw in their faces were blank stares.

Jeff and I have had the distinct pleasure, on many occasions, of giving talks and doing book signings at assisted-living facilities, where we have met many wonderful people. The timing of these events presents a few challenges—among them, making sure we avoid lunchtime and, in some cases, trying to keep participants engaged before their nap time. I do not use a microphone when speaking, so, when I notice a few vacant stares, I know that I have to speak louder.

It is truly a very rewarding experience to meet and greet these individuals who have invited us into their homes. In particular, I would like to mention Jean, a resident who was especially gracious to us. She invited Jeff to her room to read some of the poetry she hoped to publish some day.

✕ ✕ ✕

THREE THINGS TO REMEMBER

When giving advice to a younger audience, there are three things that I always ask the children to promise me:

1. To never follow strangers.

2. To never dig in the sand with their hands, but to instead use shovels or scoopers. (I show them all the dangerous items hiding in the sand, like sharp fishing hooks and pieces of rusty metal.)

3. Lastly, to have patience while detecting (a characteristic that kids are not generally known for).

YOU ARE RICH

A GROUP OF FIVE-YEAR-OLDS attended one of my presentations, and afterward, one of them remarked, "You are rich!" I smiled. He was referring to my treasure chests, which are overflowing with coins, miniature cars, and jewelry. Then, from the back of the group, another youngster added that he was rich as well. Obviously, he was too young to be a metal detective, but I later found out that his father is a professional athlete, so I guess he may have been correct with his statement.

THE TREASURES
KEEP COMING

THE SHEER WEIGHT OF MY TREASURES always amazes my audiences. I recently had to purchase a dolly in order to transport all my coins, jewelry, and other items. It has become a challenge to just lift one of my chests containing coins with denominations less than a quarter. I will eventually have to make the difficult decision of the fate of my treasures and how they will be distributed among my seven wonderful grandchildren.

I am contemplating giving each one their weight in coins. The downside to this solution is that it might encourage overeating by each child, and their parents would not be very happy with my method of passing on their inheritance.

ONE READER'S REACTION

ONE OF MY READERS received my book as a gift and, after reading it, wrote to tell me that she truly enjoyed the stories. I mentioned in the book that I have rarely, if ever, seen a female metal detective, but knew that women would have the stamina required to perform the task. She said she was living proof of this and hoped someday our paths would cross.

A VERY TIMELY GIFT

ON ONE MILD CHRISTMAS DAY, I decided to go detecting at a local beach—just a way to pass some time while waiting for a good home-cooked meal. Only two people were in sight, which wasn't surprising since most families were home celebrating the holiday.

The couple asked me about my hobby, and of course I could not resist telling them about my book.

Both looked at each other as if light bulbs had switched on over their heads.

They explained that they were on their way to a relative's house for dinner and had no idea of what to bring as a gift. I always carry a supply of books in my car, and so I presented two books to them as gifts, immediately solving their problem of finding what they called "the perfect present."

That day was very special to me. The chance meeting on the beach became a memorable event in my life as a writer.

SELF~PUBLISHING ≠ SELF~PROMOTING

ALL AUTHORS, whether self-published or trade-published, wish to get copies of their books in the hands of as many readers as possible. It quickly became obvious to me that I had to be my own advocate. I doubt many individuals escaped my promotion of the book. My children, in particular, seemed to roll their eyes whenever they heard me talk about it. Jeffrey was the exception—he was as enthusiastic as I was!

Soon enough, I realized that after exhausting my personal contacts, I would need to reach a larger audience. What better venue than a library? The result was a few speaking engagements at local libraries, which generated sales. Then came visits to local bookstores and businesses I frequented. This strategy also proved to be highly successful. There were rejections along the way, but my efforts, for the most part, paid off.

ODDS AND ENDS

OFTEN, AT MY PRESENTATIONS, I am asked why I have dollar bills, golf balls, and plastic toys in my collection. My detector itself of course only locates metal objects, but on many occasions I find other items simply lying on the sand. I certainly could have accumulated enough plastic shovels to start my own construction company, but opted out of taking those particular treasures off the beaches; I left them for my little friends to find and put in *their* treasure chests. As for the dollar bills, these are rare finds, and are displayed at my shows just to pique the audience's curiosity. And it works!

RATTLESNAKES
AND BEES

MY GOOD FRIEND AND CLIENT DON NELSON asked if I could join him for a business meeting that would require us to stay in Northern California for a week. The area was popular many years ago for gold mining and includes the towns of Weaverville, Whiskeytown, Redding, and Denny. The region is now known as the Emerald Triangle because of the proliferation of marijuana growers that make up the majority of the population. Permission to explore any private property is a MUST.

One fringe benefit of the trip for me would be time for metal detecting in a new setting: a creek bed. Prior to this, I had exclusively worked on sandy beaches, and so this was an entirely new experience. Don had arranged for me to work with the very sophisticated Minelab Quattro MP detector, which distinguishes between coins, silver, gold, and other miscellaneous metals. This particular detector also works under water, an option that I never had with my own piece of equipment.

I made my first attempt in the Indian Creek section of the Emerald Triangle with Don and friends Brad and Rick. Rick was especially experienced in detecting in the area, while Brad was just starting out on his search for treasures.

Reaching the creek bed was not easy, since we had to descend a steep decline, while keeping on the lookout for rattlesnakes and loose boulders. After

Me, the Metal Detective, as Goldfinger.

searching for a few hours, my detector alerted us to a rock surrounded by weeds, indicating there was possibly gold nearby. Rick pulled the weeds off, and Brad and I started panning for gold. Much to our amazement, stuck under that rock were two gold nuggets weighing eight grams, with a total value of approximately $450 to $550! Rick said it was simply beginner's luck, but Don and I could not have been more excited.

The following day, we were off to find more gold, but this time Brad stayed back, while Sophie, a visitor from New Zealand, took his place in the treasure hunt. We eventually came back to Indian Creek, slowly descending the hills to the creek bed with our eyes focused on the ground for rattlesnakes. I grabbed a branch for support and quickly realized that I had disturbed a bees' nest. Sophie and Rick were well ahead of Don and me, but they ran back upon hearing our screams.

We tried desperately to fight the bees off, but were both viciously attacked. Each of us ended up with dozens of bee stings, which took weeks to heal. But that didn't stop us in our search for gold that day! After the attack, Don saw a shiny object glistening in the water.

Sophie waded in and retrieved a Buffalo nickel that dated back to 1925. Rick and I rushed to the area with our detectors and had multiple hits, not only in the water, but also on the bedrock and hillside surrounding the site. The nickels came one after another, all apparently from the same miner's stash lost more than ninety years ago. In total, we found twenty-five nickels, all from the same time period. Even Rick, the local, experienced metal detective, was quite amazed at our find.

Several hours later, Don realized that his phone was missing, so we circled back to the area of the bee attack. At the time of the attack, Don had been wearing a pullover sweatshirt with pockets and had immediately flung it off, attempting to ward off the bees. His phone, pen, and loose cash went flying along the creek bed.

Sophie was a real trooper and wanted to go down to the creek and try to find the phone. As she watched Don's dollars floating on the water, she amazingly spotted the pen and phone.

He was so grateful that he offered her the reward of a dinner that she will never forget; she had been traveling extensively since she left home and Don spared no expense, offering her anything on the restaurant's menu, including bottomless glasses of wine. We all vowed to return each year for an annual treasure hunt and continue our search for gold.

(As an aside, the whole area surrounding our discovery is particularly rich in gold-mining history. It seems everyone has a story of finding valuable gold nuggets exceeding several hundreds of thousands of dollars!)

Unlike metal detecting on beaches, where the pace is leisurely and the treasures are the fascinating people and friendships I find, searching for gold in creeks can be dangerous and grueling, but also financially rewarding— many a millionaire has been made by discovering gold. The invention of metal detectors in 1881 proved invaluable in the search for this precious metal. One suggestion for anyone who wishes to mine for gold in the Emerald Triangle is to get the property owner's permission . . . or rattlesnakes and bees will be the least of your worries!

✖ ✖ ✖

THE DISCOVERY OF THE BUFFALO NICKELS in California brings attention to the questions posed by many as to the face value versus fair market value of many of the coins that I have found over the years.

The Barber dime, the silver-content coins, the Buffalo nickels, and foreign coins all exceed their face values. At the time of this writing, I would estimate that the coinage in my treasure chests amounts to several hundred dollars in value.

At the top of my list of most favorite finds are the Barber dime and the Buffalo nickels. The circumstance behind finding the nickels was by far the most unusual and exciting experience in all my years of being a metal detective.

THE REVIEWS

ALL THE REVIEWS OF MY FIRST BOOK, *The Metal Detective,* have earned five stars on Amazon (at the time of this writing). Authors are very aware of the importance of how their readers rate their books, and it is satisfying to know that so many enjoyed my first attempt at writing.

The many smiles and good wishes I received at speaking engagements were certainly a source of pride for both Jeff and me. The two of us make a good team at these talks, with Jeff explaining the editing process, while I concentrate on giving the audience an overview of the writing process and promotional efforts on my end.

So many parents have told me that *The Metal Detective* has inspired their children to take up my hobby. In addition to children, quite a few adults have also become detectives as a result of my book. My goal has always been to tell my story to as many people as possible and to share the wonderful experiences that this hobby has given to me. I am pleased to have been the inspiration for so many individuals.

AMONGST
MY READERS

WILLIE NELSON, OWEN WILSON, Woody Harrelson, Dave Dombrowski, and several of my retired professional athlete clients now have my book in their libraries. As I have mentioned many times, Don and Joy Nelson have been an integral part of so many aspects of my life that it is impossible to put into words how appreciative I am of their encouragement when it came to promoting my writing. I will always be grateful to them.

THE INCREASING
INTEREST IN THE HUNT

THERE IS A GROWING INTEREST in the field of treasure hunting, as detecting equipment becomes more and more sophisticated. Several television series based on treasure hunting currently vie for viewership and are successful in their attempts to gain massive audiences.

Oak Island (mentioned in my first book), off of Nova Scotia, Canada, is a dangerous island where several deaths have occurred over the years, and it is the site for the TV series *The Curse of Oak Island*. Snake Island, off the coast of Brazil, is the locale for *Treasure Quest*, a series in which treasure hunters search for buried gold and ancient artifacts on an uninhabited island known for one of the largest populations of deadly snakes. And *Detectorists* is a British comedy based on a club of metal detectives who are constantly in search of treasure.

All of these successful television series have one thing in common: the public's persistent fascination with finding out if a treasure hunter will be able to locate that lost mother lode.

"Find anything good today?" is the question that beachgoers always ask me, and that same question is on the minds of the television viewers.

I have been tempted to contact actor Robert De Niro and offer him the lead in a movie based on the experiences I have written about in my books, but for some unexplained reason, my wife, Myrna, has discouraged me from doing so. Most likely it is jealousy on her part of my being portrayed by someone famous. Unfortunately, there really is nothing in my writings that would attract Sally Field to play the wife of a successful metal detective.

ORDERING FOOD TO GO

I TAKE GREAT PLEASURE in ordering food to go. When asked by the person behind the counter for my name, the "Metal Detective" is always my answer, rather than "Alan." This, of course, brings a smile to the individual waiting on me.

Once, when my order was ready, a waitress yelled out over a very crowded restaurant, "the Metal Detective!" and everyone within hearing distance looked at me when I raised my hand. Perhaps they thought I was working the area searching for criminals and was simply ordering my food while on break.

(It should be noted here that Myrna tries to avoid any eye contact with me and simply leaves my side as quickly as possible when I pick up my order.)

Often, when I am meeting someone for the first time, I also introduce myself this way. At the time of this writing, I am strongly contemplating legally changing my name, which could have a negative effect on my marriage, since Myrna would, in all likelihood, start divorce proceedings.

A NEEDLE IN A HAYSTACK

THE "POLAR PLUNGE" on New Year's Day on Cape Cod was very exciting, not only for the masses of people swimming for charity on a forty-degree day, but for me as well.

Several months prior, I had found a rare Thomas the Tank Engine toy buried in the sand. The train, however, was missing a magnetic taillight, which decreased its value. Much to my surprise, the only discovery the day of the Polar Plunge was the missing taillight! This little piece is the size of a thumbtack, and the chance of finding it was like finding a needle in a haystack.

That day will always stand out among my metal detecting memories, not only because of what I found, but also thanks to almost getting frostbite.

A REAL SHARK
ON THE BEACH

NEVER, EVER DID I EXPECT to encounter a real shark on the beach while searching for treasures, but much to my surprise, it did in fact happen. While I was detecting on a Florida beach, I heard a voice asking me to come over to discuss my detector.

Immediately, I recognized the shark: Kevin O'Leary from the show *Shark Tank*. Of course, I was happy to talk with him, and I explained to Kevin that I, to a lesser extent, am a TV celebrity of sorts and would be more than willing to share my valuable time with him and his family.

Kevin, also known on the show as "Mr. Wonderful," mentioned that he had always been intrigued by the workings of a metal detector, and he asked my advice on what type would be best suited for him, since he was considering taking up the hobby.

We sat for quite a while discussing my treasure hunting, my book, and the fact that I had dealings in the past with fellow "shark" Mark Cuban, in my role as a CPA.

Kevin took my business card. I believe he will purchase a copy of my book *The Metal Detective* and attempt to negotiate a deal with me worth, possibly, millions of dollars. On the other hand, after he buys a metal detector, there may very well not be enough money in his coffer to purchase the book!

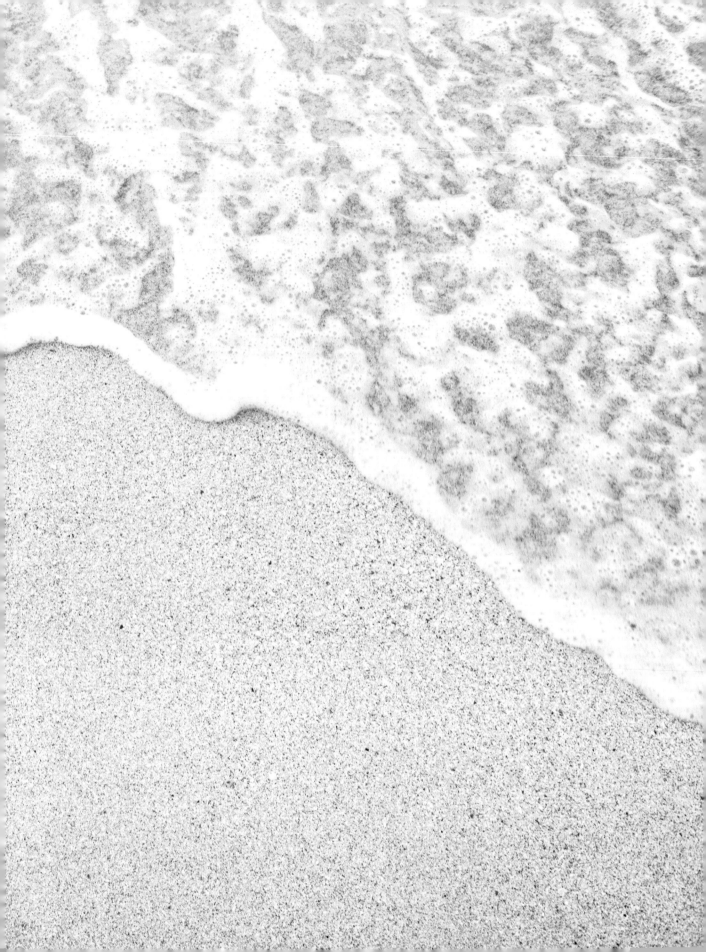

ABOUT THE AUTHOR

A LAN ROTHMAN followed in his father's footsteps, becoming an accountant and tax preparer, in a practice that specializes in working with professional athletes from all corners of the sporting world. Rothman married his childhood sweetheart, Myrna, and together they have four grown children and seven grandchildren. While their children were growing up, it was not unusual for a client/player to be seated around the Rothman family dinner table. In recent years, metal detecting has become Rothman's favorite pastime. His desire to share his experiences with as many people as possible was the driving force behind these two books-within-a-book, as well as his first book, *The Metal Detective*.

A BOOK
WITHIN
A BOOK

When I decided to write another book,
I vacillated between writing a book geared to the younger
generation versus the adult readers that my first book attracted.
Why not do both? I thought. Thus, a book within a book.

This is how Melvin, the main character in
The Junior Metal Detective, was born. My hope is that generations
both young and old will enjoy this unique idea.
Now, close the book, turn it over and around to meet Melvin.

THE END

Later that night, when they met up again, it was decided they would name the boat after their new good friend and champion of adventure, Mr. Frownface. The name they came up with was the "E. Z. Fortune-Finder."

Their good deed had been rewarded, and another name was born that day: Mr. Frownface was now known as "Mr. E. Z."

FROM THEN ON, countless fun days were spent out on the boat with Mr. Cooper giving lessons on safety, seamanship, and how to share the duties of maintenance and cleaning—as well as taking turns captaining the vessel! Best of all, Mr. E. Z. was no longer alone—he joined them for beach parties and birthday celebrations—and, for the rest of his life, Mr. E. Z. would be the group's very best find.

THE GROUP all gasped at the same time, speechless. Nodding sincerely, Mr. Frownface handed the keys and a piece of paper to Melvin, the leader of the young treasure hunters, and explained that this was their reward for finding his precious and priceless ring.

Once the children got over their shock, they learned that the keys were for a new outboard motor and the paper was to show that the boat now belonged to them! (Although, of course, Mr. Cooper would be their captain until they were old enough to venture out on their own.) Isaac, Henry, Caroline, Sloane, Melvin, and even Zoe jumped up and down with excitement and huddled around old Mr. Frownface, unable to contain their joy.

Then they all ran home to tell their parents about their good fortune.

BUT THIS TIME, instead of going in the front door, the old man led them toward his fenced-in backyard. There, they saw a very big something under a tarp. No one could guess what it was. The old man had a sly and twinkling grin on his face. Slowly, he pulled back the tarp, and . . . ta-da! A beautiful, brand-new boat appeared before their eyes!

A COUPLE OF months later, on a sunny and warm summer day, all the treasure hunters were on the beach, when Mr. Frownface waved them over to his home.

Scoop and his friends gladly welcomed the opportunity to visit with their new friend, and they decided to take a break from their detecting.

"Come, kids, see what I have for you!" Mr. Frownface urged excitedly as they approached his property.

MELVIN LOOKED to his buddies and nodded to them to join Mr. Frownface in his house. They sat down in the living room, and it was like meeting a whole new person. In fact, they ended up having so much fun that everyone thought they should do it again!

Mr. Frownface, who was now smiling, offered the children a reward, but they refused. Their parents long ago had taught them that no rewards should be accepted for lost items returned to their rightful owners. And the children were happy just to know that the beach in front of the spooky home would no longer be off-limits but, rather, a gathering place for the start of each day's treasure hunts.

✕ ✕ ✕

ALL OF A SUDDEN, tears sprang to the old man's eyes. "This is the ring that my dear, late wife, Matilda, gave to me on our wedding day, sixty years ago. It was a symbol of the love we shared for so long. But I lost it while walking on the beach several years ago, and I was certain I'd never see it again."

Mr. Frownface looked up and wiped a tear from his cheek. "Please, children, come in and sit down with me and my dog, Zoe, and my cat, Bella, and have some milk and cookies," he said gratefully.

A WEEK WENT BY before Melvin and his friends gathered enough courage to return the ring. Finally, one day after school, everyone met at Melvin's house to get the ring and make their way, fearfully, to Mr. Frownface's house.

Feet dragging, they went up the creaky front steps and knocked on the door. From inside, they heard the dog bark and the cat hiss. Caroline and Henry were frightened and turned to leave.

But Melvin had summoned some bravery and was determined. "No!" he said. "We made it this far. We have to do it."

But before the friends could discuss it any further, the heavy door swung open and a tall, dark figure appeared.

"What do you want?" demanded Mr. Frownface. "And what are you doing on my porch?"

Melvin quickly reached into his pocket and held up the ring. "Um, hello, sir. We found this while we were metal detecting."

THAT NIGHT, Melvin showed his parents the prized finding. They looked in awe at what was clearly a very special piece of jewelry.

Mrs. Cooper inspected it more closely, and gasped when she saw the initials. "E. Z. F.—Elijah Zachary Frownface! It must be! Melvin, you'll have to return this to Mr. Frownface."

Melvin gulped. Just our luck, he thought. He knew the ring had to be returned, but he did not look forward to the idea of confronting old Mr. Frownface for any reason. "Maybe, uh, you guys could give it to him?" he asked his parents.

"Now, Melvin," said Mr. Cooper, "you kids found Mr. Frownface's lost ring. I'm certain he'd appreciate you all returning it." But Melvin wasn't so sure. . . .

✗ ✗ ✗

THEN ONE DAY while metal detecting, Isaac yelled out to everyone, "Hey, guys! Check this out!" Melvin, Caroline, Henry, and Sloane ran to Isaac, and they peered down at something sparkling by his feet.

"Is it pirate's gold?" asked Caroline.

"No, but it looks like a ring," Isaac said as he slowly and carefully lifted a gold ring from the sand. On the inside of the ring were engraved the letters "E. Z. F." Isaac handed Melvin the ring to put in the treasure chest for safekeeping.

BUT IT WASN'T ALL bounty and booty, as the pirates like to say. While combing the beach, they always had to avoid one area: Mr. Frownface's home. Mr. Frownface lived in a spooky, ramshackle house that was probably twice as old as he was. It was no secret that Mr. Frownface hated beachgoers getting near his property, so the children stayed away. Melvin, however, felt bad for the old man, whose only friends, it seemed, were his dog and his cat.

Several months went by, and the treasure chest was still only half full. Melvin and his friends were losing hope that their dream of buying a boat would come true anytime soon.

EACH DAY, MELVIN would walk the beach with his trusty metal detector and his friends—Isaac, Henry, Sloane, and Caroline. His friends started calling him "Scoop," because he was always using his scooper to sift through sand. Even Melvin's parents thought the nickname was cute and started using it.

"Hey, Scoop, what did you find today?"

"Oh, just the usual stuff—bottle caps, a few pennies, a toy car . . ."

Eventually, all of Melvin's friends convinced their parents to buy them their own metal detectors, and they hatched a plan. They would all pool their findings to save up for their ultimate goal: a new boat. Little by little, as the five friends kept searching the sand, Melvin's treasure chest began to fill.

THE NEXT DAY, Melvin went with his dad to an antiques shop that sold all kinds of interesting things. In a corner, hidden behind some umbrellas, was a wooden chest that Mr. Cooper knew would be perfect for holding Melvin's treasures. They bought it and took it home.

THE TWO BOYS went straight to Melvin's house from school and dragged the dusty gifts out of the closet. They headed out onto the sand and, within minutes, the metal detector starting beeping loudly. The boys got down on their hands and knees and used Melvin's scooper to dig. To their amazement, they found a quarter! Then came a fishhook, a bottle cap, and a penny. After an hour of searching the sand, they had found enough money to buy their candy.

That night at dinner, Melvin was so excited; he could hardly wait to tell his parents about his good fortune. "That's terrific, Melvin!" Mr. Cooper said. His parents were especially happy that their son had a new hobby to keep him busy outside in the fresh air.

✕ ✕ ✕

"MELVIN, LOOK! I've found a way for you to look for treasure on land," Mr. Cooper proudly said as he handed Melvin a shiny, new metal detector and sand scooper.

At first, Melvin was pretty disappointed with the gifts, and he left them to collect dust in his closet. Then one day, Melvin and his best friend, Isaac, needed money to go to the candy store. Aha, Melvin thought. Maybe this metal detector will come in handy after all!

MELVIN COOPER lives in a house on the beach with his parents, Owen and Emma, in the seaside community of Goldnugget. Mr. Cooper is the captain of a commuter ferry, and Mrs. Cooper greets passengers in the galley kitchen and sells them snacks.

Mr. Cooper always hoped that someday he would have his own boat. He and Melvin would talk about how they would search for sunken treasure on ships that had met an untimely end. Unfortunately, the dream of owning a boat never became reality.

But one day, Mr. Cooper had an idea. He thought that Melvin might be satisfied with a different way of hunting for treasure.

THE JUNIOR METAL DETECTIVE

The furthest thing from nine-year-old
Melvin Cooper's mind was that a
simple gift from his parents would lead
to the fulfillment of a dream . . .
and a lasting friendship.

by Alan Rothman

Edited by Jeffrey Neal Rothman

Illustrated by Daniela Frongia

SMALL BATCH BOOKS

AMHERST, MASSACHUSETTS